1. Tower
2. Pinnacle
3. Weather-vane
4. Gargoyle
5. Bell Louvres
6. Scratch Dial

7. Wes
8. Gra
9. Por
10. Ni
11. Pa
(room

18. Headstone
19. Yew Tree
20. Lych-gate
21. Table Tomb

A Ladybird Book
Series 649

This is a companion book to 'What to look for inside a Church' and tells the meaning of, and the reason for many of the things you will see in the churchyard and as part of the outside of a church building.

For much of the information on church bells in this book, the author is indebted to Canon Gilbert Thurlow of Norwich Cathedral.

What to look for OUTSIDE A CHURCH

by P. J. HUNT
with illustrations by
RONALD LAMPITT

Publishers : Wills & Hepworth Ltd., Loughborough
First published 1972 © *Printed in England*

The Church and its Site

In olden times, the site chosen for a church was often on top of a hill. Everyone could see it, and it was 'above' other buildings, as befits the 'House of God'. It had to be in a position which could be easily reached by the local people, as often it was a place of refuge from enemies as well as a place of worship. Sometimes the tower was used as a look-out post on which warning beacons were lit.

Because the church tower could easily be seen, it was the obvious place for a sundial or, later, the church clock, in the days when these were the only means by which the local population could tell the time.

A parish church was usually built with local stone, this being the most durable and easily obtainable material. The size of a church, and the lavishness of its decoration, was a sign of the wealth of the local population. For example, in the Middle Ages the wool trade brought great wealth to parts of the Cotswolds, and wealthy merchants paid for additions and extensions. That is why we can often see large and beautiful churches in what are today small towns and villages.

There is no reason why the design of a modern church should imitate that of old churches, however magnificent these old buildings might be. Each age must make its own contribution to the art of church building, bearing in mind that the worship of God is its main purpose.

0 7214 0317 4

Lych-gates

The lych-gate is the roofed gateway of a churchyard, 'lych' being the old English word for 'corpse' or 'body'. Thus the word 'lych-gate' really means 'corpse-gate'.

If you look carefully at the design of the lych-gate, you may find that a cross has been included somewhere in the structure.

At the lych-gate the coffin used to be rested on a table to await the arrival of the clergyman who was to take the funeral service. The first part of the service took place between the lych-gate and the church. The clergyman always led the funeral procession into the church, and he still does so. This is because he is the representative of the Church which is commending the soul of the dead person to God.

Before the coming of motor cars, coffins were carried by men who might have had to walk considerable distances. These bearers were glad to rest at the lych-gate, sheltered from the rain, and in some lych-gates you may see the seats on which they rested.

There are not many lych-gates dated earlier than the 17th century, but you may find a number which have been rebuilt.

Lych-gate

The Churchyard

The churchyard is the land which surrounds the church. It has been consecrated by a bishop and is sometimes called 'God's acre'. ('Consecrated' means 'set apart as sacred'.)

A cemetery is not the same thing as a churchyard, because there is no church in it, although many cemeteries have small chapels attached to them.

All parishioners (people living in the parish) have a right to be buried in the churchyard, and the cemetery is used when the churchyard is full.

Animals are not allowed to graze in a churchyard, and no-one may fell or plant trees unless he has first obtained the permission of the Parochial Church Council, the 'incumbent' (usually the vicar or rector), and the Archdeacon. Misbehaviour in the churchyard can be punished by law.

The incumbent must also give permission before gravestones are erected and no grave may be dug within 12 feet of the church. Burials do not normally take place on Sundays, Christmas Day, Ascension Day or Good Friday, unless there are very special reasons.

Churchyards were busy places in olden times, and parishioners used to make some solemn agreements there. They rightly thought that pledges made in so sacred a place were specially binding.

Churchyard Crosses

The cross is the symbol of Christianity, and in some churchyards you will find a large cross or the remains of one.

These crosses were originally used as outdoor preaching places. The preacher stood beside the cross, in the open air, and used it as a sort of 'visual aid' to his preaching. He would point to it and remind the people that Christ had died for them on the cross.

The cross was also used as an important 'station' (a stopping-place where prayers might be said) in church processions; sometimes the cross was also used as the place from which public pronouncements were made.

At one time, before tombstones were common, it was believed that the churchyard cross served as a single memorial to all the dead.

Missionaries used to set up crosses and use them as preaching places before churches were built. Some of these early crosses were very beautifully carved and had sculptured figures on them.

You may also see a cross on the outside of a church building. A cross was often placed at the point of the gables for instance, and many modern churches have a large cross on the face of the building.

Crosses are also carved on some of the gravestones in the churchyard.

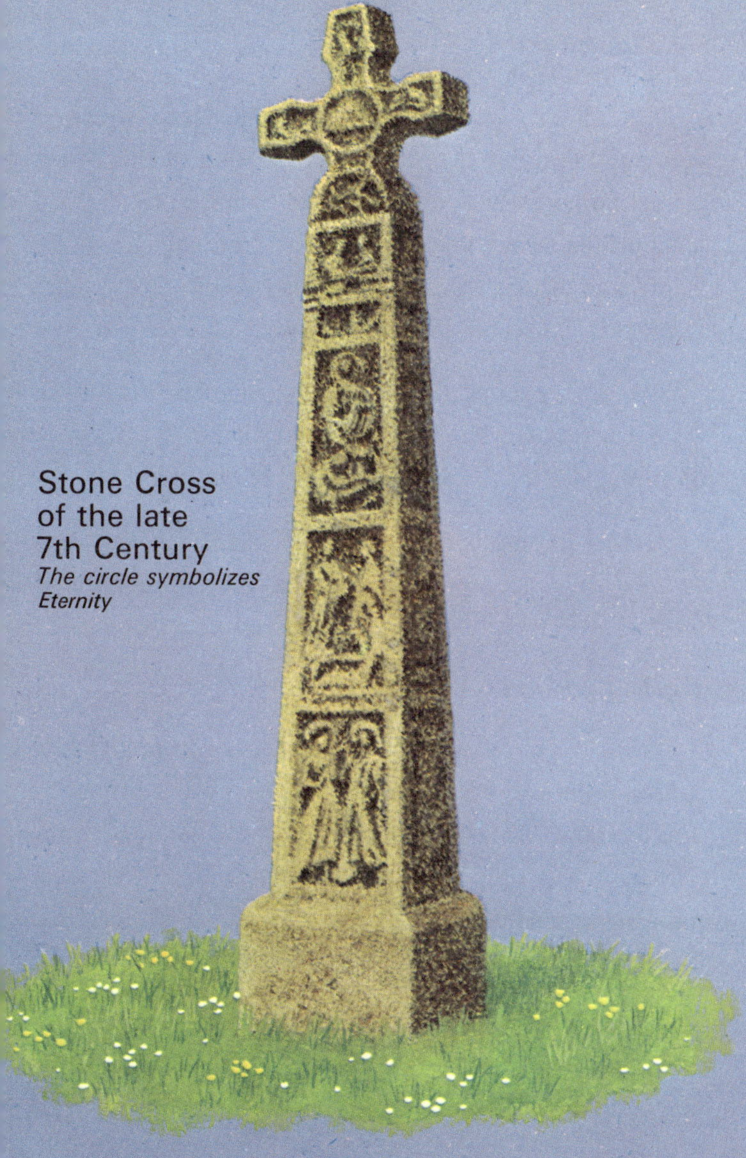

Stone Cross
of the late
7th Century

The circle symbolizes Eternity

Types of Crosses

Not all crosses are shaped in the form which is generally familiar to us today, for not all of them have arms. Some early ones, known as 'lantern crosses' had a figure or statue at the top; some had a niche in the shaft, and others, especially the early Anglo-Saxon ones, were rather like tall pillars and were richly carved.

The most common form of cross, shaped †, is known as a *Latin cross*, but there are many other types which you may see, both outside and inside the church.

A cross standing on three steps is called a *Calvary cross* or *graded cross*, and the steps have been thought to represent Faith (top), Hope and Charity.

The *Greek cross* has all its arms of equal length.

The *Maltese cross* is a black cross of eight points on a white ground. It got its name because it was adopted by the Knights of Malta and dates back to the times of the Crusades when the Hospitallers of St. John of Jerusalem used it for their emblem. (Compare the emblem of the St. John's Ambulance Brigade today.)

The *anchor cross* was used by the early Christians in the catacombs, and this is thought to date back to the days of Ancient Egypt.

Latin Cross
Greek Cross
Maltese Cross
Calvary Cross
Anchor Cross

Gravestones and Headstones

If you look at the inscriptions on the headstones in the churchyard, you will often learn a little of the history of the families who have lived in the district. You may find the same surname over and over again.

The headstones serve a similar purpose—that of memorials to thc dead—as do the wall tablets and memorials which are to be found inside the church. Outside, the gravestones and headstones are often of stone, but sometimes they are of marble or granite, which can be unfortunate if it does not harmonise well with the material of which the church is built.

You may find some graves raised above the ground and quite monumental in size; these are table tombs and are rather like the altar tombs which are found inside some churches. Sometimes they have large canopies erected over them, but this is usually when the grave is that of an important personage.

On the gravestone or headstone is carved the epitaph. The older ones particularly are often interesting to read. Some may be in rhyme and carry warnings to all who read them; others may tell something of the life of the person buried there.

The letters 'R.I.P.' stand for the Latin words 'Requiescat in pace', meaning *May the dead person rest in peace.*

RIP
Lyeth the Body
EPHEN FRITH of
f Deptford
STEPHEN
H FRITH
ho Died
an^ry 1733
ars.
Take heed all ye who look on here,
As ye are now, so once I were:
As I am now, so must ye be;
Therefore prepare to follow me.

Sundials and Scratch Dials

A sundial is a very old instrument for measuring time. There are quite a number still existing in our churchyards today.

Perhaps one of the earliest forms of instruments for measuring time is the 'scratch dial', which was so called because it was scratched or cut onto the outside wall of the church or other prominent building. Before clocks came into common use, these dials were used to note the times of church services.

You will usually find sundials standing on a pedestal or column. The dial itself—in both sundials and scratch dials—is marked out in lines radiating from a central point and which represent hours, half-hours, and so on. At the central point is a metal rod, called a gnomon or style, which casts a shadow onto the dial. When the sun is strong enough, you can tell the time by noting where the shadow falls on the dial.

The church sexton used the dial to tell him at what times to ring the bell for services, but he could only do this during daylight hours when the sun was strong enough for the gnomon to cast a shadow. In dull, wintry weather the sundial was not much help.

Some scratch dials are puzzling, because they have marks where no shadow could ever rest. They may have been used to indicate service times, or merely as an artistic decoration.

Sundial

Scratch Dial

Watch Boxes

During the late 18th century, and at the beginning of the 19th century, a small structure called a watch box was sometimes put up in the churchyard.

Its purpose was to provide shelter for the men who were put on guard at night in order to prevent body-snatching. You may wonder who would want to dig up a body and take it from the churchyard. The answer is that at this period of time, the science of medicine was growing and bodies of recently-buried persons were needed so that they might be dissected and studied. Medical students, in particular, were prepared to go to great lengths to obtain a body on which to work.

Sometimes ruffians made quite a living by opening graves and selling the bodies to teachers of anatomy, even though they knew they would be severely punished if they were found out.

Naturally, people were very much against this custom of body-snatching, and so it was necessary to have the churchyard guarded during the hours of darkness.

In 1832 an Act was passed which made it necessary to have a licence before a body could be dissected, and this helped to stamp out the practice of stealing bodies.

Trees in the Churchyard

You will often find yew trees in a churchyard, and they are usually very old; sometimes they are older than the church itself, and may have formed part of the groves in which pagans worshipped in pre-Christian days.

The yew is a slow-growing and very long-lived tree, so it has been looked upon as a symbol of immortality and therefore a suitable tree to be planted in the place where people are buried.

However, there were other reasons for having yews in churchyards. Its thick, close growth protected the church building against gales and storms; indeed, it has been said that a post of yew will outlast a post of iron. As the yew is poisonous to animals, farmers kept their beasts and cattle away from it, and so the yew guarded the church.

During the 13th and 14th centuries, the longbow was used very successfully in warfare. It was made from the wood of the yew.

Branches of yew were often used to represent palms in the Palm Sunday processions, and were also used to decorate the church at Easter and other times. In medieval times, Palm Sunday was sometimes known as Yew Sunday for this reason.

Yew

Shrubs in the Churchyard

Some of the shrubs, trees and flowers which you may find growing in the churchyard, or near to it, have long been thought to have a symbolic meaning. They remind us of things connected with the Christian faith. Here are a few of them:

Holly. The prickly leaves of the holly tree have often been thought of as a reminder of the crown of thorns which Jesus wore when He was crucified. The red berries are like drops of blood, and serve to remind us that Christ's blood was shed for us. Thus the holly tree has come to be known as a reminder of the Passion of Christ.

Laurel. This is another evergreen shrub which has interesting associations. It has long been thought of as an emblem of victory and distinction, in the art world for instance; so we get such phrases as 'look to your laurels', and 'resting on one's laurels' when one has given up striving after further rewards.

In the days of the Roman Empire, victors in athletics and successful generals had their heads crowned with a garland of laurel leaves.

The laurel then may remind us of the great victory of Christ over sin and death.

Holly

Laurel

Flowers in the Churchyard

Clover. This three-leaved plant is a very obvious symbol of the Holy Trinity. Each leaf has three parts, which are not three separate leaves, but one leaf. So likewise, God is God the Father, God the Son, and God the Holy Ghost; yet He is not three Gods, but one.

It is said that St. Patrick used a clover leaf as a visual aid when he was teaching about the Holy Trinity.

Lily of the Valley. This little flower, with its white blossoms is a symbol of purity and humility, and it is often associated with Mary the mother of Jesus.

Violet. This is another humble little flower, which you may find growing under the hedges; it is sometimes thought to remind us of the humility of Jesus when He came down to earth as a man.

Christmas Rose. This is a hardy little plant with a white flower which blooms at Christmas time. Thus it has been thought of as a reminder of the Nativity.

The Daffodil and the Lily. These beautiful flowers remind us of everlasting life. Though the bulbs look dead when they are placed in the ground, new life springs within them and they blossom into beautiful flowers. So our churches are decorated with such blooms especially at Easter time.

Daffodil
y of the Valley
Red Clover
Madonna Lily
Christmas Rose
Violet

Towers and Spires

At the west end or in the centre of most church buildings you will see either a tower or a spire.

The church tower reminds us of the times when the church was used as a post of defence against enemies. Square, solid and strongly built, it was an ideal place from which archers could shoot their arrows. Occasionally, very old towers were built in a circular shape. In some churches you may find that the tower is detached from the building to which it belongs, but usually is joined on. Cathedrals and very large churches may have more than one tower.

The spire is a pointed structure which rises above the tower in the form of a tall cone or pyramid. Many people think of it as a finger pointing upwards to the heavens. Some spires are covered with rectangular pieces of wood called 'shingles'. Others may be covered with tiles, lead, or occasionally copper.

Many towers contain a *clock* but, before clocks were common, people relied on the church bell to peal the hours. Clocks with dials were not much used until the 14th century. The hours were sometimes struck by cleverly-designed mechanical figures called 'jacks'.

Church with Tower

Church with Spire

Weather-vanes

At the top of the church spire there may be a cross or perhaps a weather-vane or weather-cock.

A weather-vane (sometimes spelt 'fane') is a device for showing which way the wind is blowing. It is a thin plate of metal or wood which pivots on a vertical spindle according to the direction of the wind. You may also see the points of the compass (north, south, east and west) incorporated as part of the weather-vane, and these are usually marked by the letters N, S, E, W cut out in metal.

The weather-vane is often in the form of a cock, and this reminds us of Peter's denial of Jesus. Jesus had warned him that, before the cock crew twice, Peter would deny Him thrice. (Mark, 14, v. 30).

Vanes have been in use for hundreds of years. Sometimes they were cut into ornamental forms, such as heraldic devices; others were in the form of small flags which were sometimes pierced to represent a family coat-of-arms.

On some old church buildings, you may find figures of birds or animals forming vanes which were placed on the tops of pinnacles and other high parts of the buildings.

Weather-vanes

Belfries

The belfry is the bell-tower, or 'campanile', of a church; usually it forms part of the church building, but in some places is detached.

The belfry is also the name given to the room in the tower in which the bells are hung. Underneath it, is the ringing chamber.

In smaller churches which do not have towers, you may find a bell-turret, sometimes called a bell-gable or bell-cote, at the west end of the church. This usually contains one bell, but sometimes it has two, and in very rare cases three. Many are Early English in style, though a few date from Norman times.

Sometimes you may see a smaller bell-turret at the eastern end of the roof of the nave. This was for the Sanctus Bell, which was rung at a certain point (the elevation of the Host) in the service of Mass or Holy Communion. The Sanctus Bell was generally made of silver, and its ringing during the service helped to recall people's wandering thoughts and reminded them that a most solemn part of the service had been reached. People outside the church knew when they could especially join with fellow Christians inside the church in sending up a prayer to God.

Church Tower cut away to show Belfry

Bells

Nearly all churches have a bell or bells, the chief purpose of which is to call the people to worship. Before clocks became common, church bells were sometimes used to peal the hours. Some bells have been in use for six hundred years. They are cast in 'bell-metal' which is an alloy of copper and tin.

In the Middle Ages, the curfew-bell was rung to warn people to put out all fires. Nowadays bells ring out on happy occasions such as weddings, and on sad ones such as funerals.

The bells are housed in the belfry, and the place where the bell-ringers ring the bells is known as the ringing chamber. If you look up, you will see that the 'windows' at the top of the tower do not have glass in them. Instead they have openings (louvres) in the stone-work so that the sound of the bells may travel out over the surrounding town or countryside.

Church bells are often very large and may weigh several tons. Many of them have messages cut on them in the metal. They may be messages such as 'I to the Church the living call, and to the grave do summon all', or 'May Jesus Christ be praised'; or the message may give a little of the bell's history, such as 'I was cast at Gloucester'.

If you climb the tower, you must NEVER climb in among the bells, and NEVER touch the ropes. This can be very dangerous. Only go up the tower with a guide.

A Church Bell

Porches

The entrance to most churches is through a porch which is often found on the south side of the building.

In medieval days, the porch was a most important place; the Baptism Service began there and part of the Marriage Service was held there too. There, also, penitent sinners were given absolution (i.e. forgiveness) from their sins before entering the church.

As the church was often near the market-place, the porch was used as a place in which to carry out civil business. Legal agreements and solemn promises were made there and, because it was a part of the church, it was a reminder that the agreements were made before God and so must be honoured.

Sometimes the coroner held his court there and public notices were put on display. You may still see some of these in the church porch today.

If there are stone seats in the porch, this may mean that it was once used as a school. Some porches have an upstairs room where books, documents, wills and accounts were stored. This upper room was sometimes used as a place for the priest to sleep, so that he could be readily available to take early services for travellers.

The Church Door

The door of an old church is usually very strong, because in olden times a church was a place of refuge as well as a house of prayer.

Most churches have more than one door; there is often one on the north, south and west sides of the building. The one on the north is sometimes called the 'Devil's door', because it was left open during a baptism service, so that the evil spirit thought to be in a child could escape.

In many churches the doorway protected by the porch is on the south side of the building, though where the porch is on the north, it may be because the Manor House was on that side of the building.

Early Saxon doors usually have a semi-circular arch over them; Norman doorways are generally round-headed too and deeply recessed, due to the thickness of the church wall. They often have a 'dog-tooth', zig-zag type of decoration around them.

Doorways in the Early English style are generally curved to a point, while those of the Decorated style of architecture often have a richly ornamented canopy over them. Those of the Perpendicular style usually have a flatter arch within a square frame.

Some old church doors have a 'cat-hole' near the bottom of the door. This was for the church cat to come and go as he pleased, for he often did a useful job in keeping down the church mice which damaged books and materials in the church.

Late Norman doorway. St. Nicholas Church, Barfreston, Kent.

More about Church Doors

Saxon church doors were usually plain and simple pieces of workmanship, but from Norman times onwards, they were often much more decorated.

Strongly made doors to keep out invaders were constructed of thick oak boards in two layers; these were placed vertically on the outside and horizontally on the inside, and were fastened together by iron nails which often had ornamental heads.

Norman doors also had beautifully made wrought iron hinges, locks and latches, which were fine examples of the work of the medieval smiths. During the Middle Ages, the hinges were a prominent part of the door and were usually ornamented with decorative scrollwork. In Early English architectural work, this iron scrollwork often covered almost the whole of the door.

In olden times, some church doors had knockers; if a fugitive felt he had been wrongly accused, he would run to the church and take hold of the knocker. No-one could then touch him. There is a very fine example of a sanctuary knocker at Durham Cathedral.

Sanctuary Knockers
nd old Lock and Latch

Niches in the Church Wall

A niche is a recess in some part of a wall, or other place in a building, into which a statue or image is usually placed. Sometimes the niche may contain a vase or some form of ornament. Church walls, especially those built in Norman times, were often very thick, and this allowed plenty of room for a niche to be carved in them.

Often you will see a niche over the church door which contains a statue of the church's patron saint (i.e. the saint to whom the church is dedicated); occasionally some other saint may fill this niche.

In some churches, the niches are found in groups of two or more, and perhaps these may all be placed under one larger arch.

Niches are either semi-circular or, occasionally, square at the back, and often have canopies carved over them. Sometimes there is a small pediment (a triangular-shaped part) above and small columns or pilasters at the sides, but often they are quite plain.

Niche

Gargoyles and Corbels

A gargoyle is a projecting stone waterspout which was often used in Gothic architecture. Its purpose is to throw out the rainwater from the gutter of the church roof, and so to get it clear of the walls of the building itself.

Occasionally gargoyles are quite plain, but more usually they are carved in grotesque forms of animals, birds and humans, and often these are very ugly or sometimes quite amusing. The carvings have open mouths out of which the water drains.

The ugly ones were said to represent human vices and sins, and they were looked upon as a warning to all who entered the church to leave their evil thoughts outside and so to come into the church in a fit frame of mind to worship God.

A corbel. This is a carved piece of stone or wood, projecting from a wall to support weight (e.g. an arch). Here again, quaint heads and figures were often used in their design and the workmen must have let their imaginations go in the likenesses they represented.

Gargoyles

Buttresses, Parapets and Chains

A buttress is a projection from a wall and is designed to give the wall additional strength and support. The weight of the roof of a building tends to push the walls outwards, and so buttresses strengthen them.

As well as giving additional strength, buttresses help to relieve the monotony of plain walls. In Norman churches they were usually the same breadth and thickness from ground to top.

Later buttresses were divided into sections and were also ornamented with niches and other carved decorations.

Parapets. A parapet is the low wall at the edge of a roof. It can be of various designs; sometimes it is plain, sometimes it has battlements or panels, or other forms of ornament.

Chains. Occasionally you may find a piece of chain attached to a wall—or the place where a chain has been. These were provided for the use of drovers so that they could tie up their cattle while they were in the church attending the service.

Parapet

Norman Buttress

14th Century Buttress

Chain for Cattle

Wall Markings, Votive Crosses and Graffiti

The word 'graffiti' means drawings or writings scratched on a wall. It may also refer to a form of decoration made by scratching through the plaster in order to show a different coloured surface underneath.

If you look carefully, you may see such markings on the outside walls of some old churches. Marks were sometimes cut by the stonemasons as a way of putting a signature on their work. Some marks were made by pilgrims who paused at the church on their journeys elsewhere; some of these marks are thought to have been connected with the making of a solemn vow, and so they are called 'pilgrim marks' or 'votive crosses'.

On some churches there is a sign, shaped rather like an arrow-head, cut into the stone. This is known as a bench-mark, and has been made by a surveyor. If you refer to a large-scale map of the district, you will find the height of the ground above sea-level is marked at that point.

In some places, the name of a farm or large house is cut into the churchyard fence. This was so that the occupiers of the houses so named would know that they were responsible for repairing that part of the fence.

Graffiti

Stocks, Pillory, Ducking-stool and Mounting Block

There are several things which may be found near the church or village centre, and from which we may learn of life in bygone days and the way people dealt with wrongdoers.

Stocks. This structure consisted of two pieces of wood into which wrongdoers were fastened by their legs. The holes in the stocks were large enough to hold a man's ankles securely when the two pieces of wood were locked together. Offenders had to endure the ridicule of the villagers and were targets for rotten fruit and vegetables.

The Pillory consisted of a post on which was a wooden frame with holes for the neck and wrists. Offenders received similar treatment to those in the stocks.

Ducking-stool. This was a chair attached to a long plank or pole. Offenders were fastened into the chair, which was then ducked or dipped several times in the local pond.

Mounting Blocks or Mounting Steps. These were most useful in the days when the horse was the chief form of transport. They were used by people who were not very agile, to help them mount their horses. A mounting block was placed near the churchyard for the use of people who rode their horses to church.

Stocks
Pillory
Ducking-stool
Mounting Block

The Clergy House and the Tithe Barn

The Clergy House. From about the 14th to the 16th centuries a house for the priest was often built near to the church, so that it was convenient for him to get to the church in order to take services. There are not many of these original houses left, but those that still exist are often very fine buildings.

Nowadays the parish priest's house is usually called the vicarage or the rectory, and it is still built near the church whenever possible. There is no difference between the work of a vicar and a rector today, but the different titles date back to times past when the rector collected tithes (taxes) and the vicar did not. (See Tithe Barn.)

Old vicarages and rectories are often big, rambling houses which are difficult to run without a full staff of servants; a number of parishes are now demolishing these old houses and erecting up-to-date dwellings instead.

The Tithe Barn. In medieval times the clergy sometimes received tithes in the form of grain or fodder instead of money. These tithes in kind were put in a storehouse called a tithe barn. Some tithe barns were very large and a few still exist today.

Clergy House

Tithe Barn

CONTENTS

	Page
The Church and its Site	4
Lych-gates	6
The Churchyard	8
Churchyard Crosses	10
Types of Crosses	12
Gravestones and Headstones	14
Sundials and Scratch Dials	16
Watch Boxes	18
Trees in the Churchyard	20
Shrubs in the Churchyard	22
Flowers in the Churchyard	24
Towers and Spires	26
Weather-vanes	28
Belfries	30
Bells	32
Porches	34
The Church Door	36
More about Church Doors	38
Niches in the Church Wall	40
Gargoyles and Corbels	42
Buttresses, Parapets and Chains	44
Wall Markings, Votive Crosses and Graffiti	46
Stocks, Pillory, Ducking-stool and Mounting Block	48
The Clergy House and the Tithe Barn	50